The Vegan Soup Collection

AMARPREET SINGH

Copyright © 2015 by Amarpreet Singh

The right of Amarpreet Singh to be identified as author of this Work has been asserted by her in accordance with sections 77 and 78 of the Copyright, Designs and Patents Act 1988.

All rights reserved. No part of this publication may be reproduced, distributed, or transmitted in any form or by any means, including photocopying, recording, or other electronic or mechanical methods, without the prior written permission of the publisher, except in the case of brief quotations embodied in critical reviews and certain other non-commercial uses permitted by copyright law. For permission requests, write to the publisher, addressed "Attention: Permissions Coordinator," at the address below.

Publisher - The Thought Flame

info@thethoughtflame.com

www.thethoughtflame.com

Table of Contents

Introduction 1

Chapter One: What Does It Mean To Be Vegan? 3

Chapter Two: How The Vegan Diet Can Protect You From Heart Disease and Stroke 7

Chapter Three: How A Vegan Diet Can Help Boost Your Emotional and Mental State of Mind 13

Chapter Four: Delicious Vegan Soup Recipes 18

Conclusion 30

About Us 32

Author 34

Introduction

There are those out there that claim that being Vegan is a lifestyle choice, and the truth of the matter is that this is the truth. If you are reading this book then you are either a vegan or want to become a vegan in the near future.

The importance of being fit and healthy is now being brought into the spotlight since the cases of obesity and food related illness have been on the rise at the start of the past decade. Instead of treating obesity or an unhealthy lifestyle that is something that is just bothersome, it should be treated more as an epidemic as it affect millions of people world wide. Many of these "victims" range in age from elderly to toddlers.

Instead of focusing on all of the negative aspects of unhealthy eating, this book is aimed at highlighting the positive aspects of healthy eating. We will look in depth on how to feed your body with the food it deserves considering our bodies are more our friends than anything. As our friend we only want the best for our bodies and do not to force food into it that is only going to harm it in the long run.

This book focuses on the positive aspects of living a vegan lifestyle and how it can help you to not only become healthier, but how it can help you to lose weight in the process.

So, what are you waiting for? Let's get started!

Chapter One: What Does It Mean To Be Vegan?

Have you ever looked at the Earth as a whole and seen how truly blessed it is with the types of delicious food that grows from its depths? The Earth itself is abound with the most succulent vegetables you will find, the juiciest fruits that you will find and the most nutritious grains you will find anywhere. Is it no wonder many people out there wonder why humans don't eat more food that grows from the Earth.

This particular class of food has been proven to be not only the healthiest food that we humans can eat, but its has been proven to be incredibly delicious, if made the right way.

What most people do not realize is what this diet can do not only to your physiological state, but your mental state as well. A Vegan diet enhances our physical body as well as your spiritual and emotional self as well. What does this mean? It pretty much means that you will live a much healthier, happier and much more peaceful life while on the Vegan diet.

So, what is a vegan?

A vegan is a person who permanently and strictly only consumes an all plant diet. Vegan is a person who not only consumes plant materials, but avoid all dietary or other products that derive from any living creature. A vegan usually does not believe that any animal, whether it is poultry, dairy or marine, should be harmed in the process of providing us with nourishment. To a vegan, all life is sacred, even those of animals and as such all life should be treated with the respect it deserves.

What Does A Vegan Diet Consist Of?

A true and organic vegan diet usually comprises of such foods such as fruits, seeds, nuts, legumes, grains and of course vegetables. Anything and everything that comes from the earth itself and can be grown in one's backyard is pretty much free game for a vegan.

The History of Veganism

The whole concept of both a vegetarian and a vegan diet is a much wider issue than many people realize. It is not just about eating a healthier diet and living a much healthier life. It goes deeper than that and its roots can be traced back to the very dawn of time for every human on the planet.

If you want to see exactly where a Vegan diet was born, you need to look back to the very birth of humanity itself and you can find a variety of history books on the subject matter.

The point of the matter is that no matter what a person is only as mentally, physically and emotionally healthy as the food they consume. The healthier the food, the healthier the person. It is that simple.

Chapter Two: How The Vegan Diet Can Protect You From Heart Disease and Stroke

The heart is the most important organ in the body today. Think about it, can you really live without your heart? However, as important as this organ is, it is still surprising that many people do not take special care of it the way that they should. More people today die from heart attacks and strokes than they do from most cancers. The main cause for these heart attacks is not stress or a unhealthy family history. In fact, it has to do with what we eat.

How The Vegan Diet Can Help Protect Your Heart

Let's take a closer look at this for a second. When a waxy substance known as plaque begins to build up inside the walls of your coronary artery, you will begin to develop a dangerous condition known as atherosclerosis. Of course this is not something that happens over night. This dangerous plaque builds up over the course of many years and comes from two primary sources: grease and meat.

Over time the plaque will begin to line the walls of your arteries and once this condition reaches a dangerous level, the artery itself can rupture or if it is large enough it can block all blood flow to your heart. This is known as a true heart attack. This type of attack deprives your heart of the very thing it needs: oxygen. Once that happen the heart muscles begins to die and will continue to die unless the situation is reversed as fast as possible.

This condition has been occurring as far back as we can remember. In the 1960's scientists began to experiment to come with solutions to this problem. Instead of finding a "cure" for a heart attack they found an interesting connection between the consumption of meat and heart attacks. It was even written in the American Medical Association journal in 1961 that by following a vegetarian or vegan diet, people could reduce the risk of heart attacks and development of heart disease by up to 97%.

When you consume an all meat diet, you are consuming high levels of negative cholesterol and saturated fats. These substance are then deposited straight into the arteries of your heart where they build up dangerously over time. On the other hand, when you follow a vegan diet, you are consuming such a low level of cholesterol and saturated fats that practically nothing will build up in the arteries of your heart. The simple fact is that a vegan diet equals a strong and healthy heart.

You also have to keep in mind that a vegan diet is high in nutritious fiber, which can be found commonly in many vegetable sources, grains and legumes. Fiber is one substance that helps to keep your heart healthy as well as your entire digestive tract. A vegan diet is also high in Vitamin C and important antioxidants, which all help to sustain a healthy heart as well.

How The Vegan Diet Can Help Protect You From A Stroke

When you think of a stroke, think of it as a heart attack but in your brain instead. A stroke is essentially when a blood clot forms in an artery inside your brain, blocking all important oxygen from reaching that section in your brain. When this happens the cells within that particular part of the brain begins to die of, resulting in critical brain damage.

Regardless of where the damage begins to occur in the brain, this brain damage that is suffered is traumatic. There are many things that your brain is responsible for and that you may not be aware of when you do them such as controlling your memory, control the movement of your body or controlling your speech. To be honest, nothing about a stroke is fun and in severe cases people have been known to die from this kind of attack.

So, what causes a stroke? It all comes down to nutrition and how well you have been eating throughout your life. Taking in harmful substances such as cholesterol and saturated fats increases the risk of developing these harmful clots in your brain and the more you consume, the more likely you are to suffer a stroke in your lifetime.

How will a Vegan diet help combat this condition?

Well, a Vegan diet is filled with healthy and important nutrients such as essential fatty acids, anti-oxidants and important minerals. All of these things help make this diet anti-inflammatory, which can help to remove excess stress on your body in the long run. This can help create an environment that is highly conductive, meaning that it can help prevent the formation of harmful plaque and clots in the long run.

Chapter Three: How A Vegan Diet Can Help Boost Your Emotional and Mental State of Mind

When you look at how you feel emotion, feel desires and have feelings, you need to take a step back and look at yourself from a different perspective. When you look at these things you need to look at yourself as an astral self and your body is an astral body. This "astral" body is the invisible part of your body that surrounds you. While I know this makes it sound as if you are some crazy shroom trip, just bear with me.

How A Vegan Diet Boosts your Emotional State of Mind

Now, the more purer your astral body, the more refined your actual body is. This astral part of yourself is the instrument that helps to control your emotional energy and your emotional state of mind. This emotional energy helps to develop power within yourself and helps to bring out the true beauty and wisdom of your very soul.

When it comes to eating the food that you need, it is important to keep in mind that the finest parts of the food that you eat are consumed by your astral body and can actually refine its appearance around you and thus influence your very emotional and mental state as well.

When you eat a meat-only centered diet, it pollutes your astral body and even jeopardizes the relation between your astral self. The animals that are slaughtered to feed us humans often live in a constant state of fear. For some people they believe that fear still lingers in the meat that we consume and hence contaminates our astral selves. When you eat meat that is contaminated with fear, many people believe that you are more prone to experiencing those emotions as well as experiencing anxiety and sorry.

However, consuming a solely vegan diet helps to promote more positive emotions such as joy, happiness, a sense of calm and even love.

How A Vegan Diet Can Boost Your Mental State of Mind

Our minds are perhaps the most complex thing about us. Our minds are wrapped in a delicate structure and surrounded by a mental aura that is invisible to the naked eye. The main function of our minds is to serve as an eternal connection between the human body and our souls, not just to help our body functions normally on a daily basis.

Now when we consume food, the most delicate and finest pieces infiltrate our minds and aura, influencing our very thoughts and feelings. The fact of the matter is that whatever food we consume, no matter what it is, becomes a part of our very minds and influences the way we think and feel on a day-to-day basis.

When you eat a diet primarily consisting of meat, your mental state of mind becomes very sense and course, vibrating at a frequency that is very low. What does this all mean? It simply means that the meat pollutes your mind and can intoxicate it in a very negative way. It can sabotage any calm feelings that you may have, inhibit your responsiveness to a situation and even reduce the clarity of which you think.

Now, when you consume a diet consisting of primarily vegan ingredients, your mind becomes in tune with the very light of your true self. A vegan diet consists of pure and refined components, all associated with a healthy state of mind. A vegan diet can enhance the clarity of which you think, increase its effectiveness and render your mind into an instrument that is as powerful as your human body. If you want a clear and calm mental state of mind, eating only a pure and healthy vegan diet is the way to go.

Chapter Four: Delicious Vegan Soup Recipes

Hearty Zucchini and Red Pepper Soup

This dish will satisfy you unlike any other vegan dish that you come across. It is hearty and savory, making this a dish that you will want to make all of the time.

Serves: 4 Servings

Ingredients:

-¼ Cup of Olive Oil

-½ Cup of Rice, Basmati

-1 Eggplant, Sliced Into 1 Inch Cubes

-5 Cloves of Garlic, Chopped Finely

-3 Tomatoes, Fresh and Diced Into Small Pieces

- 1 Cup of Onions, Chopped Finely

- 1 Red Bell pepper, Chopped Into Small Pieces

- 1 ½ Cups of Water, Warm

- ¼ tsp. of Red Pepper Flakes

- ¼ Cup of Basil, Fresh

- ½ tsp. of Salt and Pepper For Taste

- ¼ Cup of Parsley, Fresh and Chopped Finely

- 1 Sprig of Rosemary, Fresh and Chopped

- 1 Cup of Wine, Marsala

Directions:

1. Place your eggplant into a medium sized colander and sprinkle with your dash of salt and pepper. Slice up your eggplant and sauté in a pan with some oil until it is slightly brown in color. Then stir in your onion and sauté until the onions are translucent. Next add in your garlic and sauté with your eggplant and onion

for about 2 to 3 minutes.

2. Then stir in your rice, tomatoes, water, red pepper flakes, some additional salt, pepper, zucchini and red bell pepper. Make sure your cook your mixture over medium heat until it reaches a nice rolling boil and then reduce the heat. Allow to simmer for about 45 minutes or until all of your vegetables are tender.

3. Remove from heat and stir in your rosemary, basil and parsley until thoroughly combined. Serve while still piping hot.

Potato and Creamy Broccoli Soup

This is one of the perfect soup recipes to make for you to enjoy during the cold winter months. It is both savory and extremely creamy, leaving you with a delicious soup that you will want to make again and again.

Makes: 4 to 5 Servings

Ingredients:

-3 Cups of Broccoli, Sliced Into Florets and Chopped Finely

-2 Potatoes, Peeled and Chopped Finely

-1 Onion, Large In Size and Finely Chopped

-3 Cloves of Garlic, Minced

-1 Cup of Cashews, Raw

-1 Cup of Vegetable Broth, Low Sodium

-4 Cups of Water

-3 Tbsp. of Olive Oil, Extra Virgin

-½ tsp. of Nutmeg, Ground

Directions:

1. Soak your cashews in a bowl covered with water for at least 4 hours. Then drain the water and blend your cashews with your vegetable

broth until it is smooth in consistency. Set aside.

2. Gently heat up your olive oil in a large sized saucepan over medium to high heat. Cook your chopped onions and minced garlic and for at least 3 to 4 minutes until the onions are tender.

3. Next add in your broccoli florets, chopped potato, ground nutmeg and water. Cover your mixture and bring to a rolling boil. Once boiling reduce the heat and allow your soup to simmer for at least 20 minutes, making sure that you stir it from time to time.

4. Then remove your soup from heat and stir in your cashew mixture. Blend until your mixture is smooth, return to your pan and cook until it is completely heated through. Remove from heat and serve immediately.

Creamy and Savory Potato Soup

If you are a fan of potato soup, this is one recipe that you are going to love. It is extremely creamy and very filling, making it one recipe that you will soon fall in love with.

Makes: 4 to 5 Servings

Ingredients:

-6 Potatoes, Medium In Size and Sliced Into Small Sized Cubes

-1 Leek, White Part and Finely Chopped

-1 Carrot, Fresh and Chopped Finely

-1 Zucchini, Peeled and Chopped Roughly

-1 Celery Stalk, Fresh and Finely Chopped

-3 Cups of Water

-1 Cup of Coconut Milk

-3 Tbsp. of Olive Oil, Extra Virgin

-Dash of Salt and Black Pepper, For Taste

Directions:

1. Gently heat up your olive oil in a deep saucepan and sauté your onions for at least 2 to 3 minutes.

2. Next add in your chopped potatoes, carrots, zucchini and fresh celery and cook for at least 2 to 3 minutes, making sure to stir constantly.

3. Then add in your water and salt and bring your mixture to a rolling boil. Then lower your heat and allow your mixture to simmer until the vegetables are fully tender.

4. Next pour your mixture into a blender and blend until smooth in consistency. Add some coconut milk and blend some more before serving.

Mediterranean Style Chickpea Soup

This is one of the best soup recipes out there especially if you are looking to change it up a bit in your kitchen. With a tangy and spicy taste, this is one recipe that will give you the kick you have been looking for.

Makes: 4 to 5 Servings

Ingredients:

-1, 15 Ounce Can of Chickpeas, Rinsed and Drained

-1 Onion, Small In Size and Finely Chopped

-2 Cloves of Garlic, Minced

-1, 15 Ounce Can of Tomatoes, Diced

-2 Cups of Water

-2 Cups of Coconut Milk

-3 Tbsp. of Olive Oil, Extra Virgin

-2 Bay Leaves, Fresh

-1/2 tsp. of Oregano, Dried

Directions:

1. Heat up your olive oil in a deep soup pan over medium to high heat and sauté your chopped onions and minced garlic for at least 1 to 2 minutes.

2. Next add in your water, chickpeas, diced tomatoes, fresh bay leaves, and dried oregano. Stir to thoroughly combine.

3. Next bring your soup to a rolling boil before reducing the heat to a simmer. Allow your soup to simmer for at least 20 minutes.

4. Then add in your coconut milk and continue cooking for at least 1 to 2 minutes more. Remove from heat and set aside to cool. Once cool enough discard your bay leaves.

5. Pour your soup into a blender and blend

until smooth in consistency. Return to your soup pot and bring back to a hot temperature. Serve immediately and enjoy.

Savory Lentil Soup

This soup recipes is packed with the all important protein that you need and filled with the great taste that will leave your taste buds tingling for more. Incredibly easy to make and absolutely delicious, this is one soup recipe that will soon become a favorite in your home.

Makes: 4 to 5 Servings

Ingredients:

-1 Cup of Lentils, Red In Color

-1/2 Of An Onion, Small In Size and Chopped Finely

-2 Cloves of Garlic, Roughly Chopped

-1/2 Of A Red Pepper, Finely Chopped

-3 Cups of Vegetable Broth

-1 Cup of Coconut Milk

-3 Tbsp. of Olive Oil, Extra Virgin

-1 Tbsp. of Paprika

-1/2 tsp. of Ginger, Ground

-1 tsp. of Cumin, Ground

-Dash of Salt and Black Pepper, For Taste

Directions:

1. Gently heat up your olive oil in a large sized saucepan over medium to high heat. Add in your chopped onions, garlic, red peppers, ground paprika, ground ginger and ground cumin into your pan and sauté, making sure to stir until the mixture just becomes fragrant.

2. Add in your red lentils and vegetable broth next. Then bring your mixture to a rolling boil,

cover, and then simmer over low heat for at least 15 minutes.

3. Then add in your coconut milk and allow to simmer for at least 5 more minutes. Then remove your mixture from heat and season with a dash of salt and black pepper for taste.

4. Next pour your mixture into a blender and blend until smooth in consistency. Pour back into your saucepan and heat over medium heat until piping hot and serve immediately.

Conclusion

In this book you have learned about the nutritional value of a vegan diet as well as the many benefits that it can hold you're your mind, body and soul. You have also learned about the many repercussions that come with consuming an all meat diet that can be very harmful to your overall health.

When it comes to dieting, eating the food that you love does not only mean to fill your belly until you are full or to satisfy whatever cravings that you have. Consuming food should serve as a means to nourish your body with the best substances possible as well as look at how food will affect your body and mind together as a whole.

It is important that you remember that the food you eat can affect you on many different levels that you weren't previously aware of before.

But by taking the step in the right direction towards following a vegan diet will not only leave you feeling healthier, but will help you live the longer and happier life that you deserve as a totally awesome Vegan.

About Us

The Thought Flame is committed to add value to its customers through various books, online courses and other resources. You can learn more about us and our books at www.thethoughtflame.com.

Don't forget to check out our amazing **online video courses** at www.thethoughtflame.com/courses/ to take your knowledge to another level.

To check out our **extraordinary collection of diet/cookbooks**, visit http://www.thethoughtflame.com/category/non-fictional/cookbooks/ .

As a part of our valued relationship with our customers, we keep providing you free promotional books, courses and other stuff on subscribing with us on our site. We have a strict anti-spam policy and assure you no spam mails will be sent to your mailbox.

To subscribe with us, visit

www.thethoughtflame.com.

Like our work and would like to say thanks?

Buy us a cup of coffee at

www.thethoughtflame.com/coffee/

Author

Amarpreet Singh is an avid learner and his passion for education has made him travel, work and study all across the world. He holds three masters degrees, including MBA, from top universities in Asia.

He is author of dozens of books, many of which are Amazon's bestseller, varying in various topics and categories. He also teaches many online courses having thousands of students across the world.

He has a keen interest in international affairs, economics, global poverty and politics, financial markets and entrepreneurship, and strives to be part of a community that shares the same passion.

He has worked as consultant with organizations like Airbus and The World Bank. He loves travelling and learning about new cultures, and has been fortunate to live/work/travel/study in countries like India, China, Korea, US, South Africa, Japan, Philippines, Singapore, Canada etc., and learn about the culture and lifestyle in each of them. To check out more of his work, visit www.thethoughtflame.com

CPSIA information can be obtained
at www.ICGtesting.com
Printed in the USA
LVHW092302061220
673511LV00035B/566